Christmas in America

in the 1700's and 1800's

A nostalgic view of Philadelphia on Christmas Eve 1773
by artist J. L. G. Ferris (1863–1930).

hristmas in merica

in the 1700's and 1800's

Christmas Around the World
From World Book

World Book, Inc.
a Scott Fetzer company
Chicago

Staff

World Book, Inc.
233 N. Michigan Ave.
Chicago, IL 60601

For information about other World Book publications, visit our Web site at *www.worldbook.com* or call *1-800-WORLDBK (967-5325)*. For information about sales to schools and libraries, call *1-800-975-3250 (United States)* or *1-800-837-5365 (Canada)*.

Library of Congress Cataloging-in-Publication Data

Christmas in America in the 1700's and 1800's.
    p. cm. -- (Christmas around the world)
  Summary: "Customs and traditions of the Christmas holidays as celebrated in America in the 1700's and 1800's. Includes crafts, recipes, and carols"--Provided by publisher.
  Includes index.
  ISBN-13: 978-0-7166-0808-0
  ISBN-10: 0-7166-0808-1
  1. Christmas--United States--History--18th century--Juvenile literature. 2. Christmas--United States--History--19th century--Juvenile literature. I. World Book, Inc.
  GT4986.A1C465 2007
  394.266309'03--dc22
                                    2006023518

Printed in the United States of America by RR Donnelley, Willard, Ohio
4th printing November 2010

Contents

Christmas in the Colonies

or the first Christmas in the New World, one has to go all the way back to the initial voyage of Christopher Columbus in 1492. The members of his expedition, crowded into three small vessels, first sighted land on October 12. He and his men spent the next two and a half months exploring the strange new islands they assumed were part of the Indies. On the morning of Christmas Day, Columbus's flagship, the *Santa María*, went aground off Hispaniola.

The explorer took this accident as a sign from God that He wanted the voyagers to start a colony on that spot. With timbers from the *Santa María*, the crew built a fortified camp, which Columbus christened *Villa de la Navidad*, or town of the Nativity. It was the first European attempt to settle in the New World since Vikings had tried to found a settlement in Newfoundland almost 500 years earlier. The Navidad colony failed as had the Viking colony. As before, other Europeans would follow.

Jamestown Colony in Virginia is thought to have been the site of the first Christmas in North America, in 1607. The English had made two previous attempts to create a permanent colony, one in Newfoundland

The Governor's Palace in Williamsburg, Virginia (opposite).

For the Puritans, Christmas was just another day.

and one on Roanoke Island. Both had ended in death and disastrous failure for the colonists. On Christmas Day 1607, it did not seem that Jamestown would succeed either. Of the slightly more than 100 pioneers who had settled on the marshy banks of the James River in Virginia the previous May, only 38 remained alive. The rest had died from famine, malaria, and attacks by Native Americans.

In December 1607, the small band of survivors was ready to abandon the colony. But even in their discouragement and misery, they took the time to hold a sim-

ple Christmas service. Even as the colonists prayed, the supply vessels bringing relief were on their way. For the first time in American history, a colony was established that would grow and thrive.

Early colonists and the thousands of brave settlers who followed them created a new land of diverse customs. These seekers of opportunity and freedom came from all over Europe. Just as they brought the tools of their trades, they brought their own ways of observing Christmas.

Compared with the jubilant ways with which Christmas is kept today, early colonial practices were something less than convivial. The Pilgrims of Plymouth Colony in Massachusetts, founded in 1620, reflected their faith's stern edict against what were called "Bacchanalian Christmases." For the Pilgrims, the first December 25 in America was just one more day of work.

A few daring souls attempted to make merry the following Christmas, claiming that to work would be against their consciences. Governor Bradford retorted that "it was against [his] conscience that they should play & others work. If they made ye keeping of it a matter of devotion, let them keep their houses, but there should be no gaming or revelling in ye streets."

The Pilgrims belonged to the Puritan sect of the Church of

England. They left their mother country to sail to the New World where, they hoped, they could practice their beliefs in their own way. As their name implies, the Puritans were determined to lead lives that were "pure" of anything that was not specifically written in the Bible. Because the Bible made no mention of Christmas parties or celebrations, in Puritan eyes, Christmas was not only immoral but illegal as well. Even mince pies were outlawed.

A decree issued in 1659 formally banned the observance of Christmas—and all other like holidays—with a penalty of five shillings to be levied against any lawbreaker. Although the decree itself was repealed in 1681, the Puritan clergy kept up their opposition in fiery sermons. For a Christmas Day service in 1712, the brimstone-sniffing minister Cotton Mather lashed out at his congregation saying, "Can you in your conscience think that our Holy Saviour is honored by Mad Mirth, by long Eating, by hard Drinking, by lewd Gaming, by rude Revelling? . . . if you will yet go on and will do Such Things, I forewarn you That the Burning Wrath of God will break forth among you."

Christmas in the Colonial era of Virginia was quite different from its counterpart to the

In Colonial Virginia, Christmas began a festive season filled with parties, music, and dancing.

Girls decorate a window with holly in preparation for Christmas in historic Colonial Williamsburg in Virginia.

or even a few weeks. In 1746, a London magazine declared, "All over the colony, an universal Hospitality reigns." And despite a nose-in-the-air comment from the aristocratic Thomas Jefferson that their activities showed them to be "in a state of deplorable barbarism," Virginians enjoyed themselves immensely.

By day the men rode to hounds or hunted the plentiful game—turkeys, ducks, pigeons, and geese—that abounded. At night, parties were made merry by music, dancing, and games that often went on until nearly dawn. Philip Fithian, a young divinity student from Princeton University who served as a tutor for the offspring of the wealthy planter, Robert Carter, left one of the few early accounts of a Virginia Christmas party.

Carter's lands sprawled over 75,000 acres (30,351 hectares) of countryside, and he could well afford to offer lavish entertainment. After breakfast—parties in Virginia started early in those days—Mr. Fithian tells of entering a large ballroom and seeing "several Minuets danc[ing] with great ease and propriety; after which the whole company Joined in country dances, and it was indeed beautiful to admiration to see such a number of young persons, set off by dress to the best advantage, moving easily to the sound of well performed Music, and with perfect regularity, tho'

North. In the Virginia colony, Christmas was not simply another day but a long, rollicking season. For landowners, the holiday season was the highlight of their rural life. The fall plowing was done, crops were harvested, and the tobacco was gathered and stored.

It was time to celebrate. The great homes of the wealthy were thrown open, and guests came and went as they pleased. No one bothered with invitations, and a Virginia hostess had no idea how many guests she might expect for dinner—or to spend the night—

apparently in the utmost disorder. The Dance continued til two, we dined at half after three—soon after dinner we repaired to the Dancing-Room again. . .When it grew too dark to dance, the young gentlemen walked over to my room and we conversed til half after six." Meanwhile the great hall was lit with hundreds of candles and "looked luminous and splendid." Everyone then returned for more dancing and parlor games until dinner was served.

Although the good squires of Virginia were English like the Puritans of the North, the Virginians chose to recreate the merry Christmas customs of Medieval England. No Puritan asceticism for them! The Yule log, usually of oak and of immense size, was cut in the forest, hauled to the house, and set afire on the hearth. The English had adopted the burning of the Yule log, originally a Norse custom, many centuries before. Among other superstitions, burning the Yule log was thought to bring good luck to the house for the year to come. Masses of holly, fir, and mistletoe decorated doors, halls, and ballrooms.

Most of Virginia's plantation owners showed special kindness to their help at Christmastime. They often gave their servants and slaves modest presents, such as a few coins, candy, or a bottle of rum. Servants and slaves, ex-

cept those who were cooks or housekeepers, were given a few days off during the holiday season.

While the Christmas celebration was largely of English derivation, Virginia's Christmas Day began with an American accent. On the morning of December 25, a great roar would resound throughout the countryside as every man fired off his musket to announce the start of the big day. Strings of firecrackers were set off, cannons would boom out a salute and, if a man had nothing else to make noise with, he would set up a clatter

Decorations made with fresh fruit commonly adorn the doorways of houses in historic Colonial Williamsburg at Christmastime.

with pots and pans from the kitchen. This noisemaking became a tradition throughout the South.

The major event of the day following brief religious services was dinner. A Virginia Christmas repast might well extend to seven or eight courses. The prestigious landowner George Washington set a holiday table typical of the era—turtle soup, oysters, crab, codfish, roast beef and Yorkshire pudding, venison, boiled mutton, suckling pig, hickory smoked ham, along with a roast turkey with stuffing. At least five vegetables, hot biscuits and cornbread, and a variety of relishes followed. For dessert there were often as many as a dozen choices—pies, tarts, pud-

dings, cakes, ice cream, and fruit. So that no one could possibly complain of hunger, dishes of nuts, raisins, and candy rounded out the impressive display.

Christmas had a special significance for George Washington and his wife, Martha. They were married in 1759 on January 6, Twelfth Night, the traditional last fling of the Christmas season. To his Virginia friends, Washington was known as a magnificent horseman who rode "with ease, elegance and power" and one of the most gracious hosts in the Old Dominion. A dinner or supper at the Washingtons' Mount Vernon estate in Virginia was the high point of any Virginian's Christmas season.

A Christmas fox hunt at day-

George Washington watches as the Yule log is brought to Mount Vernon in a painting by J. L. G. Ferris.

break commenced the holiday celebration. At mid-day, a plentiful feast was served to guests. An old Virginia saying claimed that if you lost all of your senses except that of smell you would still know when it was Christmas. Certainly the kitchen of Mount Vernon poured forth a wealth of glorious odors—mince pies, fruit cakes, plum puddings. "The joyous fumes of Christmas," they were once called. The traditionally English wassail bowl, a punch of spiced wine or ale with apples, was usually offered at some point in the festivities, as well as port and Madeira. In addition, a genial host, Washington enjoyed concocting a particularly potent eggnog from his own recipe, which was always popular among his guests. Dancing, music, and visiting that could last for an entire week followed the magnificent feast. It is no wonder that the local gentry so desired an invitation to the festivities.

Although gift-giving to tenants and servants was considered obligatory, the idea of bestowing heaps of presents upon friends and members of the family at Christmas did not come to the South until well into the next century. A kiss and a small toy were usually the limit of parental affection for children; for friends best wishes for a new year were considered sufficient.

Sadly, the happy observances of Christmas were forced to halt

A Christmas dinner at Mount Vernon Washington gives his favorite toast To All Our Friends

for a time. Angered by heavy taxes and interference by Great Britain, the colonies declared their independence from the Crown in 1776. However, winning that independence was not so simple. George Washington was forced to leave his comfortable Virginia estate and go to war.

A 15,000-man force of British regulars under General William Howe landed on Long Island in August 1776 and mauled the poorly trained troops under Washington's command. Throughout the summer and fall, Washington lost battle after

George Washington proposes a toast to his guests during a Christmas dinner at Mount Vernon in an illustration from the early 1900's.

Christmas hymns were first heard in the Old North Church in Boston in 1759.

winter quarters. General Washington decided on a desperate gamble. On Christmas night 1776, in a storm of swirling, icy snow, his tattered army boarded a flotilla of small boats. Crossing the ice-clogged Delaware River, he routed the enemy in a devastating surprise attack. Through this brilliant strategy, Washington and his Continental Army won a decisive victory. The flame of the American Revolution again burned brightly.

Christmas returned to Mount Vernon in 1783. After eight long years of fighting, the Revolution was finally won, and George Washington came home. His horse clattered up the roadway to the gracious mansion overlooking the Potomac at dusk on Christmas Eve. From all over the area came the sound of muskets being fired in salute, and huge bonfires were set ablaze in celebration. The general was back. Let the celebration commence.

Up north in Massachusetts, people continued to view Christmas as "rather a day of mourning than rejoicing" well into the 1800's. One British soldier stationed in Boston prior to the start of the Revolution noted bitterly in his diary for December 25, 1774: "Bad day; constant snow until evening, when it turned out rain and sleet. A soldier shot for desertion; the only thing done in remembrance of Christ Mass Day."

battle. By winter, Washington's troops were diminishing rapidly due to death, capture, and desertion as they retreated through New Jersey. The men were signed up only until the end of the year, and Washington was faced with the problem of finding replacements. One more defeat would almost certainly crush the Revolution. "If every nerve is not strained to recruit the New Army with all expedition," Washington wrote to a friend, "I think the game is pretty nearly up . . ."

Instead of polishing off Washington's band of hungry, ill-equipped rebels, the British halted their attack and set up

However, the harsh Puritan influence did slowly abate in New England. Some of the colonists, while agreeing that the alcoholic wassail bowl might not be proper, felt that eating a slice of mince pie or decorating their homes with a few sprigs of holly was not all that sinful. Christmas hymns were first heard in the Old North Church in Boston in 1759. Even though Christmas celebrations in Boston were still subdued compared to the revels in Virginia, Bishop Chase of Massachusetts in 1827 lamented, "The devil has stolen from us Christmas and converted it into a day of worldly festivity, shooting, and swearing." Later, the Irish tradition of placing lighted candles in the windows took hold.

Other colonists besides the English brought their traditions to the New World. The Dutch settlers of New Amsterdam, now New York City, took great delight in keeping the spirit of Christmas. They celebrated with parties and open houses. Business was suspended from Saint Nicholas Eve on December 5 all the way to Twelfth Night.

The Dutch brought with them one of the happiest of Christmas traditions. On Saint Nicholas Eve, Dutch children left their wooden shoes beside the fireplace before they went to bed, just as their parents had done in Holland. Every child knew that on that night, Saint Nicholas, or *Sinterklaas*, as he was called in Dutch, would ride up on a white horse and fill the shoes of good children with small presents, cakes, and candies. Bad children received only a switch. Then, as now, there were very few bad children at Christmas time.

The noted American storyteller Washington Irving wrote marvelous yarns about Dutch colonial life. He used the cheerful character of Saint Nicholas in several of his tales. The Dutch *Sinterklaas* eventually turned into today's familiar Santa Claus.

By 1700, thousands of German immigrants began arriving

The prosperous settlers of the Dutch colony New Amsterdam (later New York) shut down their businesses and enjoyed themselves for a whole month around Christmas.

The Moravians observed Christmas with a simple meal of buns and coffee just as they had in Germany.

in America from the Rhine provinces and settled, finally, in western Pennsylvania. It is possible that they may have brought the delightful tradition of the Christmas tree with them. According to other sources, however, Hessian troops at Trenton set up the first Christmas tree in America just before the fateful battle of 1776. The German colonists certainly brought along other Christmas customs, especially the *KristKindlein*, or Christ Child, who came on Christmas Eve, bearing presents for the children. In the 1800's, the *KristKindlein* became Kriss Kringle, an old and bearded twin of Santa Claus.

The Moravians, like the Puritans, immigrated to the American colonies to lead a simple,

godly life. The first Moravian settlement was founded in Savannah, Georgia, in 1735 as a mission to the Native Americans. Other Moravian settlements grew up in Pennsylvania and North Carolina. While the Moravians believed in a strict interpretation of the Bible, they felt that God could be worshiped with a song and good, if simple, food on the table.

The Moravians observed Christmas in America just as they had in their homeland of Germany with a celebration that included scripture, music, the lighting of candles, and food. The congregation gathered in a great hall and shared a holiday meal of buns and coffee. *Lebkuchen*, Christmas cookies made with honey, almonds, and orange peel, were a traditional favorite, as was a four-sided, wooden-based, cooky pyramid.

Moravians also brought the *Putz* to America—a version of the manger scene, but much more extensive. A Putz would often include whole miniature villages and farms, backed by snow-covered hills, lit by tiny, wax candles.

Although the major observances of Christmas in Colonial times took place in the settlements along the Eastern Seaboard, there was one recorded celebration far away on the shores of Lake Huron, now St. Ignace, Michigan. The Native Americans of that isolated outpost honored the birthday of the Christ Child with an Epiphany (Twelfth Day) pageant. Father Jean Enjalran, a French Jesuit missionary, described the proceedings.

On Jan. 6, 1679, he wrote, "All the [Native Americans], but especially the Hurons, professed a special devotion for the all-endearing mystery of our Lord Jesus Christ. They themselves entreated the priest, long before the feast day, to celebrate it in a most solemn manner." He reported that the children constructed a grotto for the Nativity scene, after which the Native Americans went to confession and attended midnight Mass.

The Hurons, having been told of the long ago pilgrimage of the Magi to Bethlehem, wanted to reenact the happening. They chose three chiefs to bring gifts of polished shells to the infant Jesus. Then a procession, led by a man carrying a star attached to a pole, marched into the church, and the ancient ritual was acted out. Afterwards, the priest carried the statue of Jesus around the village. Finally, the Hurons invited their neighbors, the Algonquins, to join them in a feast "at which they exhorted each other to obey Jesus Christ, who was the true Master of the World."

A traveler going back in time to the Colonial era in America would assuredly find some familiar customs but would also discover many more missing. Except for the lucky Dutch children of New Amsterdam, there were few presents exchanged. And even though most of the inhabitants of the new land celebrated Christmas, it was not an official holiday. At Monticello, Thomas Jefferson generally made a brief, religious note of the day and then went to work in his study.

The colorful parade of nationalities that today make up the United States had begun. Christmas customs from the Old World were rapidly incorporated into those of the New World. And then as now, the spirit was unmistakable: thanks for the past, joy for the present, and hope for the future. 🐚

A Historic Christmas

The Continental Army's historic crossing of the Delaware River the night of Christmas 1776, is captured in an oil painting that hangs in New York's Metropolitan Museum of Art. Painted in 1851, *Washington Crossing the Delaware* is Emanuel Gottlieb Leutze's best-known painting and one of the most recognized icons of United States history. Measuring more than 12 feet (3.8 meters) high and 21 feet (6.5 meters) long, this dramatic painting depicts George Washington standing in the bow of a small rowboat, the stars and stripes furled behind him, as oarsmen struggle to make headway across the icy river.

The artist Leutze used several elements, including color, motion, and proportion, to evoke an emotional and patriotic message about the crossing in this painting. Leutze used the color red to direct attention to Washington and the flag, which served as inspirational symbols for the troops.

All of the painting's elements indicate motion, except for General Washington himself, who seems as steady as a rock. The boat rocks and struggles against the wind, the currents, and the ice. Water splashes against the boat as the soldiers labor to navigate between the ice chunks. As the wind blows the flag, Washington stands erect, determined, and gazing confidently into the future as a figure of strength.

The actual size of the boat in which Washington and his soldiers crossed the Delaware—a Durham boat—was much larger than the one depicted in Leutze's painting. However, Leutze decreased the boat's size to draw attention to the physical struggle of the figures in the boat as they faced what would become a historic event.

Emanuel Gottlieb Leutze was born on May 24, 1816, in Gmund, Germany. He actually painted *Washington Crossing the Delaware* in Germany, using the Rhine River as a model for the Delaware River. Throughout his career, Leutze gained fame as a painter of American historical subjects. He settled in New York City in 1859. In 1860, Congress commissioned him to paint a mural for the United States Capitol, *Westward the Course of Empire Takes Its Way*. Leutze died on July 18, 1868. ✺

Washington and his tattered army cross the Delaware River on Christmas Night 1776 to attack British troops in Trenton, New Jersey, that is, as portrayed in Emanuel Gottlieb Leutze's Washington Crossing the Delaware *(1851).*

A Christmas Collection of Toys

In the 1700's, children did not receive a large number of Christmas presents. A single toy was all that most children in the Colonial period hoped for, though some parents, including George Washington, were more generous than others. In 1759, Washington listed the following ideas for Christmas presents for his two stepchildren, Jackie and Patsy.

A bird on Bellows
A Cuckoo
A turnabout Parrot
A Grocers Shop
An Aviary
A Prussian Dragoon

A Man Smoakg
  (a smoking man)
6 Small books for Children
1 Fash. dres Baby & other toys
A Tea Sett

Wind-up merry-go-round
from the late 1800's

Girl feeding a parrot from the late 1800's

Clown magician, circa 1880

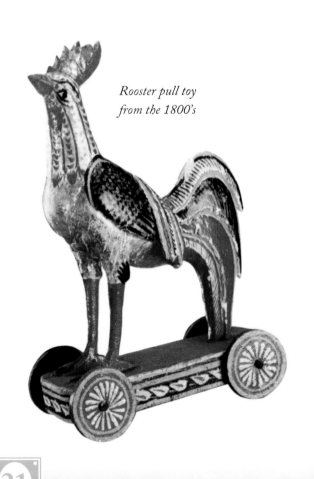

*Rooster pull toy
from the 1800's*

Doll from the 1700's

A Christmas Collection of Toys, *continued*

Although newspapers carried advertisements for toys in the late 1700's, children played mainly with each other in games and sports before the 1800's. By the 1830's, it became more common for children to receive Christmas gifts, including toys. In the mid-1800's, most children in the United States played with homemade toys or with toys imported from Europe. Parents and craftworkers made toys from tin, various fabrics, or wood. Popular toys included dolls, dollhouses, soldiers, locomotives, and ships, as well as Noah's ark sets including all of the carved, wooden animals.

Toy stores opened in Baltimore, Boston, Philadelphia, and New York City as early as 1849. However, it was not until the early 1900's that large toy factories were developed and toy manufacturing became an important U. S. industry. 🐚

Santa guiding his reindeer, late 1800's

Wooden schoolhouse,
circa 1890

Mechanical toy kitchen
from the mid–1800's

Porcelain dolls, circa 1880's

Carrying Christmas Throughout the Land

homas Jefferson took office in 1801 and immediately cast his eyes westward to the great, untamed continent that lay beyond the Mississippi River. He commissioned Meriwether Lewis and William Clark to undertake what turned out to be one of the most important expeditions in U.S. history—the exploration of the northern Louisiana Purchase territory in hopes of finding an overland route to the Pacific.

On Dec. 25, 1804, Lewis and Clark were 1,600 miles (2,575 kilometers) up the Missouri River in their winter camp near what is now Stanton, North Dakota. Like other Americans who found themselves in strange and distant places,

Lewis and Clark carried Christmas with them and celebrated it with whatever they could find at hand. On that day, Clark wrote in his diary:

"I was awakened before Day by a discharge of 3 platoons from the Party and the

A family selects a Christmas tree and mistletoe to decorate their home in the 1880's (opposite).

The Lewis and Clark expediton as portrayed by John Clymer in his 1967 painting Crossing the Bitterroot Range of the Rocky Mountains.

french [boatmen], the men merrily Disposed, I gave them all a little Taffia [rum] and permitted 3 cannon fired, at raising Our flag. Some Men Went out to hunt & the others to Dancing and Continued until 9 o'clock P.M. when the frolic ended &c."

On the same Christmas Day, a party of soldiers kept Christmas in their own style at Fort Dearborn in the Indiana Territory. The famous fort was built in 1803 near the mouth of the Chicago River in what is now the city of Chicago. Soldiers were stationed there to protect the few Americans on the fron-

tier from Indian attacks. On Christmas Day of 1804, the soldiers made time to observe the holiday. Accounts tell of how the soldiers hauled trees from a grove of evergreens north of the river back to their barracks. They feasted on wild turkey, rabbit, raccoon, prairie chicken, roast pig, and pudding blazing with brandy. Music and dancing were also part of the celebration.

Many of the early explorers of North America have left behind accounts of Christmas in the wilderness. The celebrations were less than grand. Captain John Frémont, known as the Pathfinder, used one Christmas Day to brush up on his law study with a set of borrowed books. One member of Frémont's expedition to California in 1845 noted in his diary that for Christmas dinner they had a small change in the usual menu. Instead of eating a horse, they ate one of their own worn-out pack mules.

In 1853, the U.S. government sent out a party led by Army Lieutenant Amiel Whipple to explore possible routes for a transcontinental railroad. The exhausted surveyors spent Christmas in an open camp in northern Arizona shivering in subzero temperatures. Even so, Whipple noted that the Christmas spirit burned brightly:

"The fireworks were decidedly magnificent. Tall, isolated pines surrounding the camp were set on fire. The flames leaped to the treetops, and then, dying away, sent up innumerable brilliant sparks."

For frontiersmen and pioneers, Christmas provided an opportunity to get together with others, to call a halt to their back-breaking labor and, in many cases, to let off steam. One widespread custom was the pre-Christmas turkey shoot. Not only did it provide food for the holiday table, it allowed for some satisfyingly loud noises, and brisk competition in marksmanship, too.

A well supplied party celebrates Christmas on the frontier, in the late 1800's.

An 1863 edition of Harper's Weekly depicts a family separated by the Civil War at Christmas.

Soldiers, who are often among the loneliest of people on Christmas Day, often have a special talent for keeping Christmas even under the worst of circumstances. In 1861, Confederate General Robert E. Lee, stationed in Coosawatchie, South Carolina, far from his home in Virginia, despaired of getting a proper Christmas present for his daughter. On Christmas morning he plucked a small bouquet of flowers and mailed them to her with a note:

"I send you some sweet violets that I gathered for you this morning . . . whose crystals glittered in the bright sun like diamonds, and formed a brooch of rare beauty and sweetness which could not be fabricated by the expenditure of a world of money. . .Occupy yourself in aiding those more helpless than yourself. Think always of your father."

As the United States grew during the 1800's, it became a land of many different Christmases. In each part of the country, the accent, the style, and even the language of the Christmas observance were different, but the message of charity and good cheer was the same.

In the eastern United States, the Quakers kept a very quiet Christmas. They termed it simply "the Day called Christmas." For many years they took no of-

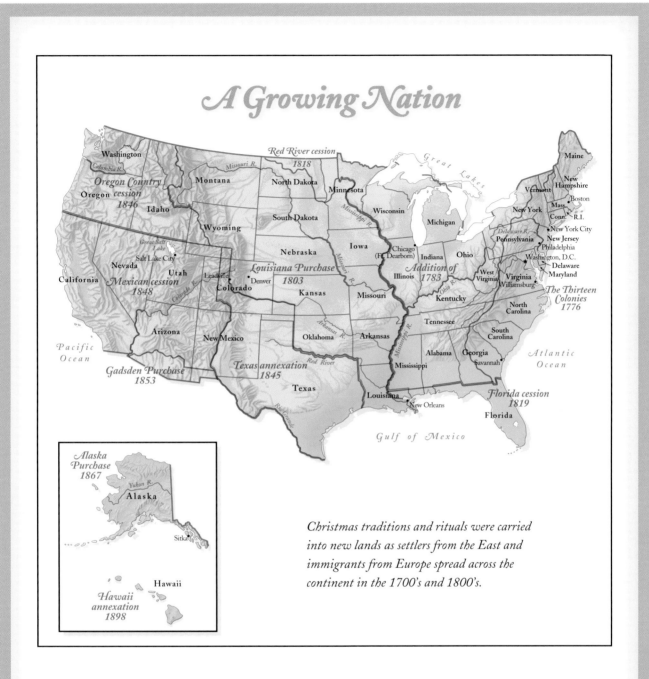

A Growing Nation

Red River cession 1818

Washington

Oregon Country

Oregon cession 1846

Montana

Idaho

North Dakota

Minnesota

Wisconsin

Michigan

Maine

New Hampshire

Vermont

Boston

New York

Mass.

Conn. R.I.

New York City

New Jersey

Philadelphia

Great Lakes

South Dakota

Wyoming

Iowa

Chicago (Ft. Dearborn)

Indiana

Ohio

Pennsylvania

Delaware R.

Washington, D.C.

Delaware

Maryland

Great Salt Lake

Salt Lake City

Nevada

Utah

Mexican cession 1848

Leadville

Colorado

Denver

Nebraska

Louisiana Purchase 1803

Kansas

Missouri

Illinois

Addition of 1783

West Virginia

Virginia

Williamsburg

Kentucky

The Thirteen Colonies 1776

North Carolina

California

Colorado R.

Arizona

New Mexico

Oklahoma

Arkansas

Tennessee

South Carolina

Pacific Ocean

Gadsden Purchase 1853

Texas annexation 1845

Red River

Mississippi

Alabama

Georgia

Savannah

Atlantic Ocean

Texas

Rio Grande

Louisiana

New Orleans

Florida cession 1819

Florida

Gulf of Mexico

Missouri R.

Mississippi R.

Columbia R.

Arkansas R.

Ohio R.

Alaska Purchase 1867

Alaska

Yukon R.

Sitka

Hawaii

Hawaii annexation 1898

Christmas traditions and rituals were carried into new lands as settlers from the East and immigrants from Europe spread across the continent in the 1700's and 1800's.

ficial notice of the day, opening their shops and working in their factories as always. Like the Puritans, the Quakers took the Bible literally. As Christmas is not mentioned in the Bible, they ignored it. In 1812, when the Pennsylvania legislature adjourned for a two-week holiday, a Quaker newspaper chastised the legislators for wasting the taxpayers' money to "draw three dollars a day for eating Christmas pies."

Pennsylvania had several interesting Christmas customs in the 1800's. Children must have particularly enjoyed a custom called "barring out the schoolmaster." A day or two before Christmas, school children would lock their teacher outside

*Children gather
Christmas trees in
a Currier and Ives
lithograph from the
1800's.*

the schoolhouse, allowing him
to get back in only if he pro-
mised to give each pupil a small
Christmas gift.

"Belsnickling" was the un-
wieldly name for another Pennsylvania custom. The German
Belsnickel was a mystical spirit
of Christmas who visited houses
just before Christmas and gave
the children toys—or switches—
depending on their behavior
during the past year.

The famous Mummers' Pa-
rade in Philadelphia held each
year on New Year's Day originated with the English settlers
of the Delaware River Valley. In
the 1700's and 1800's, costumed
and masked groups would go
from house to house on Christmas Eve presenting little plays

in return for money, or cakes,
cider, and beer.

Christmas with a French fla-
vor was celebrated in widely
separated areas. In New Orleans, the flower-scented, mild
air of the holiday season
sparkled with the customs of
Old France. Christmas lasted a
whole week for the fun-loving
Creoles of the 1800's. Families
gathered together in New Orleans, many coming from distant
plantations or small settlements
in other parts of Louisiana.

After a solemn midnight
Mass at St. Louis Cathedral,
réveillon began. Symbolizing the
wanderings of the Three Wise
Men, *réveillon* was the traditional Christmas morning feast. It
usually included *daube glacé* (a

jellied meat dish), a rich rum cake, and *Café Brûlot,* an after dinner coffee drink. Adults then stayed up and talked most of the night. The children, having hung their stockings, went to bed to await *Papa Noël's* arrival.

Papa Noël, the French Santa Claus, filled the stockings with candies and small toys. However, the real gift giving did not take place until *Le Jour de l'An,* New Year's Day. There would most likely be a *crèche,* a replica of the manger scene in Bethlehem, for children and adults alike to enjoy.

To the north, other French-born settlers celebrated Noël in somewhat similar ways. The fur trappers around the Great Lakes also kept the tradition of *réveillon.* However, their menu varied from the elegant ones in New Orleans. Roast pig, goose, beef, chicken pie, and a pastry filled with chopped beef called "bear paws" was followed by sausage, headcheese, fruits, nuts, and cake.

The Christmas customs of the Old World often took on new meanings after being transferred to America. The Norsemen burned a huge, oak log once a year to honor Thor, the

The Christmas Party, *(about 1850) by American painter Robert David Wilkie.*

Preparing for Christmas in an engraving by Winslow Homer (1836-1910).

god of thunder. In England, it was considered good luck to keep an unburned part of the Yule log all year. To the slaves in the Missouri Territory, however, the Yule log had a special significance. As long as the Yule log burned on the hearth of the big house, the slaves were let off from work. Naturally, they took time to carefully choose the biggest and greenest log fresh from the woods, and it was not unknown for them to sprinkle the burning log with water to prolong the burning time.

In Leadville, Colorado, and Denver, where mine owners had become millionaires overnight, the holiday parties were often sumptuous dinner dances where men and women dressed in evening clothes danced until dawn. Christmas trees were set up in the great houses. Along with decorations, the trees were loaded with costly gifts for all the guests.

"They think nothing of giving Christmas and New Year's presents worth from $100 to $200," said one visitor. "A nice diamond ring, pin, or a gold watch and chain" were common.

In the gold or silver camps that supplied such wealth, the miners held their own Christmas. They fired their pistols into the air and banged their tin dinner plates together to make a happy, Yuletide sound and then sat down to a dinner that was probably quite meager. One old-timer recalled a Christmas spent with two friends: "I took out of my belt two heavy (gold) nuggets and gave one to each of them. It was a poor enough gift. Gold was a common commodity with us. They'd have appreciated a hot biscuit more."

In the cattle country of Texas, cowboys celebrated Christmas pretty much the same way they celebrated everything, with a dance. As one historian of the Old West pointed out, "A round-up's close, Christmas, New Year's Eve or some purely personal achievement of local interest, all were valid excuses for going to town to visit the dance hall."

The problem was that until the late 1800's there were not many women to dance with. Many a rancher would gladly ride 200 miles (322 kilometers) just to dance with a lady. For those who could not or would not make such a long trip, the cowhands staged what were called "heifer brand" dances. A few of the cowboys would tie bandanas around their arms and take the lady's part in the dance.

One part of the West—Salt Lake City, the home of the Mormons—did not lack women, but in the first years of its settlement, the late 1840's, there was little time for any kind of dancing. The first two Christmases in Salt Lake City were bleak, as the Mormons could not afford to take time off from clearing their lands to celebrate. It was not until 1849 that 150 Mormons gathered for a Christmas dinner at the home of Brigham Young, the Mormon Church's second president who had led his people to their new settlement. As the colony became more prosperous, Christmas parties at Young's home became a tradition. Children were given toys or more useful presents like woolen scarves and mittens. Religious services were simple, and the day started with a prayer meeting followed by an exchange of gifts.

Out on the great plains of Nebraska, Kansas, and Iowa, Christmas was often a community affair, where the farming families from miles around gathered in whatever public building was available. The Christmas Eve observance that three denominations held in Iowa's Franklin County Court House in 1868 was typical. They had hoped to have a large, evergreen tree for the children, but evergreens were hard to come by on the prairie. When someone remembered a stand of tall cedars along the Iowa River, about 20 miles (32 kilometers) away, the Reverend L. N. Call and a deacon volunteered to make the trip through freezing weather to bring one back. The decorated tree, plus presents for everyone, made the day a decided success.

In the mid-1800's, Minnesota was being populated by farmers, as well as fur traders, miners, and lumbermen. Its Scandinavian settlers kept their own colorful, Old World customs, including setting out sheaves of wheat on Christmas Eve for the birds.

The Spanish influence in frontier America was far-flung, its roots dating back many centuries. All the way from Santa Fe, throughout the Southwest and up into California, the Spanish Americans practiced the customs of the past. *Los Pastores* (The Shepherds), miracle play, was acted out in many parts of the Southwest. The play was usually presented outdoors and could last as long as five hours. The basic theme was the age-old struggle between the forces of good and evil. Typically, the devil stopped and harassed the shepherds on their way to Bethlehem to visit the Christ Child, but all comes out well in the end.

Las Posadas (The Lodgings) is one segment of *Los Pastores* and was staged far more often. A procession, with many people playing various roles, acted out Joseph and Mary's journey to Bethlehem and their desperate search for an inn. Beginning nine days before Christmas, the procession went to a different house nightly. The owner at first refused admittance, but eventu-

ally let everyone in. They prayed before the manger, or *nacimiento*, and then dancing and feasting began.

Children were most fond of the *piñata*, always a big part of the festivities. It was a fragile, earthen jar, usually decorated to look like an animal and filled with candies and small gifts. The piñata was suspended from the ceiling, and the blindfolded children were handed sticks to try and break it, whereupon the candies tumbled out and the children tumbled onto them.

Some Native Americans, noting that the newly arrived Americans seemed to celebrate Christmas with more than ample feasting, referred to the holiday as the "big eating." Others called it the Kissing Day—so named from the habit of French trappers of kissing one another when exchanging gifts. Native American tribes, who already worshiped the evergreen as the "ever-living" tree, eventually adopted the Christmas tree.

The Inuit, also known as Eskimos observed their own festival of midwinter, *Sinck tuck*, with costumed folk dancing, feasting, and gift-giving. Each year, one village entertained another, and the next year exchanged the honor. European explorers brought the Christian Christmas to the people of the North. Russians who carried their Eastern Orthodox religion

to the new communities settled some areas. In Sitka, the old, English custom of "Christmas waits" was practiced by men who carried a star on a long pole and wandered through the town singing carols. Others went visiting, dressed in costumes and masks. They remained silent while their hosts tried to guess who they were.

Colorful or somber, rowdy or religious, lavish or meager, the Christmas celebrations of pioneer America all merged to form a potpourri of optimistic faith in a new country. Christmas was being kept, and slowly the traditions of many people began to blend into a national heritage with a unique character all its own. 🍥

Christmas Eve in Colonial Times, *an 1892 illustration by James S. King.*

Early American Christmas Decorations

The people of Colonial America relied on the natural materials available to them, such as mistletoe, branches of holly, and mountain laurel, to decorate during the Christmas season. Boughs and garlands made from these materials were often hung from the roof, walls, pillars, pews, pulpit, and sometimes the altar of churches.

The Christmas tree gradually became a centerpiece of most home Christmas celebrations in America during the last half of the 1800's. Americans of the 1700's decorated the interior of their homes with wreaths and garlands made from evergreens, a symbol of eternal life. Dining tables

The country squires of Virginia celebrated the Christmas season in high style as shown in an elegant holiday setting at the Governor's Palace in historic Williamsburg.

Evergreen wreaths decorate a window at
historic Williamsburg at Chrismastime.

Garlands and a fruit-laden wreath
decorate a Williamsburg house.

A reconstructed 1830 Michigan house adorned with holiday greens.

might be decorated with fruit, artfully arranged in pyramid form. However, fruit was not used in the creation of wreaths and garlands. People in the 1700's and 1800's would have considered the idea of hanging a wreath made with fresh fruit outside to rot in the cold or to be eaten by animals wasteful. Pineapples especially were considered a valuable commodity and would not have been used for purely decorative purposes. Further, most colonists did not decorate the exteriors of their houses.

It was not until the 1930's that fruit, vegetables, and dried flowers came to be used in the creation of Christmas decorations and, at that time, only in the homes of wealthier people. Louise Fisher, who was responsible for flowers and Christmas decorations at the Colonial Williamsburg restoration, is credited with creating and popularizing the first wreaths using fruit available to the colonists. She was inspired partly by the work of the Italian sculptor of the 1600's, Luca della Robia, and his

descendants. The della Robia family name became widely associated with the fruit-and-foliage swags that would influence Fisher's Christmas and door decorations in Williamsburg. Although these fruit-laden door swags, garlands, and wreaths did not originate in Williamsburg, nor did they emerge during Colonial times, they have come to be known as "Colonial Williamsburg door decorations."

The Colonial Williamsburg door decorations, which were popularized after the city's historic restoration in the 1920's and 1930's, combine elements of fruit, flowers, pinecones, wheat, and greenery.

Christmas with the First Family

When George Washington held the office of president of the United States, there was no White House in which to entertain. So George and Martha Washington often invited friends and relatives to spend the Christmas season at Mount Vernon, their plantation in Virginia. Festivities often lasted a week or two and included fox hunting and holly gathering.

On Christmas morning, they usually attended church. At midday, a plentiful feast was served to guests. The Washingtons were known for being generous hosts, and people were honored to be invited during the holidays.

The famous structure on Pennsylvania Avenue, which has housed every president since John Adams, was not a very comfortable building when it was first occupied in 1800. Set close to a swamp, the house was cold, damp, and drafty. Just to stay comfortable in its unfinished rooms, the Adams family kept 13 fireplaces constantly roaring. Nevertheless, John Adams threw the first children's Christmas party at the White House, in honor of his granddaughter, Susanna.

The party was a great success, undoubtedly helped along by the irrepressible spirit of the First Lady, Abigail Adams. The East Room was hung with greenery, cakes and punch were served, and a small orchestra played. The entertainment also consisted of caroling and lively games.

One small guest, carried away by the excitement, broke one of Susanna's brand-new doll dishes. Four-year-old Susanna retaliated by biting off the nose of her friend's doll. President Adams had to step in to restore order.

A hand-colored engraving of the White House in 1877 (opposite).

The next inhabitant of the White House, Thomas Jefferson, was a widower. Christmas would have been a lonely time for him had it not been for his beloved grandchildren. In 1805, six of them came to spend the holiday with him. Dolley Madison, wife of the then secretary of state, acted as the president's official hostess. She invited more than 100 of his grandchildren's friends to a Christmas party, which Jefferson enjoyed himself so hugely that he brought out his violin and played while the children danced. Most Christmas parties at the Jefferson White House, however, were elegant affairs. Guests dined on foods that his French chef prepared in the European fashion with exotic sauces and delicacies.

Andrew Jackson, the seventh president and hero of the War of 1812, was known as a tough-skinned campaigner. But there was a softer side to "Old Hickory." His wife Rachel died soon after his election to the presidency. Emily Donelson, his niece, acted as the White House hostess.

One Christmas week, six children visited, four of Mrs. Donelson's and two of the president's grandchildren by his adopted son. The children pestered the servants and any other adult who would listen to find out if there really was a Santa Claus. Not satisfied with the answers they were getting, 6-year-old Johnny Donelson decided to ask the president himself if Santa would come to the White House that night. The president told the boy he would have to wait and see.

The children, while hanging their own stockings on Christmas Eve, insisted that President Jackson hang one, too. The next morning, the crusty, old, former general wept as he pulled small gifts, including a corncob pipe, from his stocking, which the family had filled secretly in the night. Young Johnny, surrounded by his own pile of presents, had his answer. Santa had come after all.

The little boy had another question for his granduncle. Did Santa Claus *always* come? The president replied that once there was a boy whose mother was dead and who had never even

Guests at a Mount Vernon Christmas party in 1789 dance a lively Virginia Reel in a painting by J. L. G. Ferris.

heard about Santa. The boy had no toys at all for Christmas. It was not until years later that Johnny realized that Jackson himself had been that boy.

Jackson then proceeded to call for a carriage and went out to visit an orphanage where he personally distributed the gifts he had brought. The next day there was a merry party at the White House, replete with candies, cakes, and games. The president himself joined in a snowball fight in the formal East Room—cotton balls lightly covered with starch were used as ammunition.

At last the children, covered with "snow," bid farewell and trooped across the lawn. One guest said he thought they looked like "the fairy procession in *Midsummer Night's Dream*." Jackson shook his head. He said they made him think of the words, "Suffer the little children to come unto Me, and forbid them not, for of such is the Kingdom of God."

Franklin Pierce, who was elected president in 1853, erected the first White House Christmas tree. At the time, the ornamented "German Tree" was a fairly new innovation in the United States. However, by the end of the century, it had become the focus of most home Christmas celebrations. Today the national observance of the Christmas season does not officially begin until the president lights the giant tree on the Ellipse—the park directly south of the White House.

During the bitter days of the Civil War, Christmases with the Lincolns were quiet, family affairs. A characteristically generous act of compassion marked President Lincoln's last Christmas in 1864. On December 24, Gideon Welles, his secretary of the navy, approached the president on behalf of Miss Laura Jones of Richmond, Virginia. Three years before, she had become engaged to marry a Southerner but had gone to Washington, D.C., to nurse her ailing mother. After Mrs. Jones had regained her health, the daughter wanted desperately to return to her betrothed, but she needed presidential permission to get through the Union lines.

Welles made it clear that Miss Jones was a dedicated, Southern sympathizer. The weary president said that it was all right. "The war has depopulated the country and prevented marriages enough," he commented. As an added thought, Lincoln dated his letter December 25, so Miss Jones could have it as a Christmas present.

Over the years, Christmas at the White House has been observed in many different ways. American presidents, just as do all Americans, celebrate the holiday season by carrying on their own traditional, regional, and family customs.

The Evolution of Santa Claus

Like almost everyone else in America, Santa Claus is descended from an immigrant. One of those ancestors, St. Nicholas, can be traced as far back as the 300's.

In Europe, Santa-like characters have had many names. Father Christmas, *Sinterklaas*, *Papa Noël*, and *Kris Kringle* were just a few. In some countries, he would arrive riding a white pony, in others on a camel. One legend has him appearing on Christmas Eve, sitting on the back of a wagon drawn by a team of goats. To the children of Holland, he was somewhat stern. In Germany, he was like a judge who looked at your record and handed out rewards or punishments accordingly. In the United States, Santa Claus has generally been regarded as a jollier figure. Few children believed he would come all the way from the North Pole just to bring them a switch.

The vision of Santa Claus that captured the American imagination came from a poem, first published anonymously in the *Troy* (New York) *Sentinel* on Dec. 23, 1823. The poem is known by at least three names: "An Account of a Visit from St. Nicholas," "A Visit from St. Nicholas," and by its first line, "Twas the Night Before Christmas." Clement Clarke Moore (1779-1863), a distinguished scholar and teacher, is generally considered the author of the poem. According to tradition, Moore wrote a brief verse to amuse his children during the

A famous image of Santa Claus by Thomas Nast (opposite) *published in* Harper's Weekly *on Jan. 1, 1881.*

Painted wood Santa Claus sculpture by John Robb.

Christmas season of 1822. The poem relates the story of a man who awakens in the middle of the night and sees Saint Nicholas coming down the chimney with a bundle of presents. In the poem, Saint Nicholas is portrayed as a stout, jolly man with twinkling eyes and a red nose. He visits on Christmas Eve dressed in a suit trimmed with white fur and riding a sleigh pulled by eight reindeer.

The poem was meant only for the entertainment of Moore's family, and he initially had no thought of publishing it. Nevertheless, the poem found its way into print, and eventually, the quiet scholar became one of the most beloved U.S. poets. However, some people have claimed that Henry Livingston, Jr., a New York land surveyor who also composed poetry, may have actually written the poem.

Although American artists of the 1800's depicted Santa Claus in many different ways, the political cartoonist Thomas Nast (1840-1902) is credited with creating the present-day image of Santa Claus. Between 1863 and 1886, Nast created a series of drawings for *Harper's Weekly* magazine that represented Santa Claus with a white beard. It was Nast who depicted Santa working in his toy shop, driving a sleigh pulled by reindeer, and placing toys in children's stockings left hanging by the fireplace. 🦠

A Visit from St. Nicholas

'Twas the night before Christmas,
When all through the house
Not a creature was stirring, — not even a mouse;
The stockings were hung by the chimney with care,
In hopes that St. Nicholas soon would be there.
The children were nestled all snug in their beds,
While visions of sugar-plums danced in their heads;
And mamma in her 'kerchief, and I in my cap,
Had just settled down
for a long winter's nap,
When out on the lawn there
arose such a clatter,
I sprang from the bed to see
what was the matter.

Away to the window I flew
like a flash,
Tore open the shutters and
threw up the sash.
The moon on the breast of
the new-fallen snow
Gave the lustre of mid-day to objects below,
When, what to my wondering eyes should appear,
But a miniature sleigh, and eight tiny reindeer,
With a little old driver, so lively and quick,
I knew in a moment it must be St. Nick.
More rapid than eagles his coursers they came,
And he whistled, and shouted, and called them by name;

"Now, DASHER! Now DANCER! now PRANCER and VIXEN!

On, COMET, on CUPID, on, DONDER and BLITZEN!

To the top of the porch! to the top of the wall!

Now dash away! dash away! dash away all!"

As dry leaves that before the wild hurricane fly,

When they meet with an obstacle, mount to the sky,

So up to the house-top the coursers they flew,

With the sleigh full of toys, and St. Nicholas too.

And then, in a twinkling, I heard on the roof

The prancing and pawing of each little hoof.

As I drew in my hand, and was turning around,

Down the chimney St. Nicholas came with a bound.

He was dressed all in fur, from his head to his foot,

And his clothes were all tarnished with ashes and soot;

A bundle of toys he had flung on his back,

And he looked like a peddler just opening his pack.

His eyes—how they twinkled! his dimples how merry!

His cheeks were like roses, his nose like a cherry!

His droll little mouth was drawn up like a bow,

And the beard of his chin was as white as the snow;
The stump of a pipe he held tight in his teeth,
And the smoke it encircled his head like a wreath;
He had a broad face and a little round belly,
That shook, when he laughed like a bowlful of jelly.
He was chubby and plump, a right jolly old elf,
And I laughed when I saw him, in spite of myself;
A wink of his eye and a twist of his head,
Soon gave me to know I had nothing to dread;

He spoke not a word, but went straight to his work,
And filled all the stockings; then turned with a jerk,
And laying his finger aside of his nose,
And giving a nod, up the chimney he rose;
He sprang to his sleigh, to his team gave a whistle,
And away they all flew like the down of a thistle.
But I heard him exclaim, ere he drove out of sight,
"HAPPY CHRISTMAS TO ALL, AND TO ALL A GOOD-NIGHT.

"HAPPY CHRISTMAS TO ALL. AND
TO ALL A GOOD NIGHT"

The Man of the Season

Over the course of the 1800's, Santa Claus transformed at the hands of American artists from a tall, stern patriarch in bishop's robes into the red-suited, white bearded, prosperous-looking, tubby and jovial Santa of later years. Images of Santa Claus appeared on envelope stickers *(below)*, in magazines such as *Harper's Weekly (right)*, as well as in illustrations for children's stories and Christmas greeting cards. 🕸

An American Christmas in the 1800's

In the nation's early years, Christmas remained largely a series of local celebrations. Each community kept Christmas, or ignored the day, in its own way. Except when Christmas happened to fall on a Sunday, it was a regular working day in Boston until 1856.

The Boston public schools did not close for Christmas until 1870. It took more than 50 years for Christmas to be declared a legal holiday throughout the country. In 1836, Alabama was the first state in the Union to take legal note of Christmas. It was not until 1890 that the Oklahoma Territory followed suit.

When Christmas was observed in this land of immigrants, the celebrations were as different as the people themselves. Almost always, these observances harkened back to some European ritual. In North Carolina, two men would get under a sheet with a steer's head sticking out and cavort around the countryside as "Old Buck," whose history can be traced back to the earliest days of Christianity.

In the Ozark Mountains, where it was possible in the 1800's to hear English spoken almost exactly as it had been in Elizabethan England, the people marked Christmas Day in January. They did so in accordance with an old European tra-

Christmas at the historic Maymont House in Richmond, Virginia (opposite). Completed in 1893, Maymont was the country estate of financier James Dooley and his wife, Sallie.

dition, discarded long before throughout the rest of the world.

In Georgia, a Major Jones once tried to recapture the Scandinavian tradition of leaving presents on the doorsteps of friends on Christmas Eve. Major Jones wanted to make a present of himself to his girlfriend. He crawled inside a meal sack and had himself suspended from a hook in front of her door. It is not certain whether he won the lady in question or not. The ardent major spent a most unpleasant Christmas Eve. A dog barked at him all through the freezing night, and he got a little "seasick" as he swayed to and fro in the gusty wind.

By 1876, as the United States was celebrating its centennial, the broad outlines of what is now called a "traditional" American Christmas had formed. The early Colonial settlers might have found the celebration somewhat puzzling. But today's Americans would feel right at home at an 1876 Christmas celebration in New York City.

Then, as now, the Christmas season started early. The holiday shopping alone took a long time. Most people were members of large families, and there were a great many gifts to buy or make. The city was filled with specialty shops where one could go just to buy English linen or French lace.

A family walks home after a long round of Christmas shopping at New York City department stores in a lithograph from the 1800's.

In addition, the first of the large city department stores had appeared with a huge selection of goods. As always, shopping for the children was the most fun. German mechanical toys appeared in great variety on the shelves. Boys and girls alike particularly prized these clockwork devices, complete with moving parts. One of the more popular models was a chicken that popped up and clucked happily over a pair of painted tin eggs. Another consisted of a pair of boxers that ferociously flailed away at each other in a small ring.

Christmas in New York City was a social season as well as a spiritual one in 1876. Among the most popular holiday entertainment were Christmas ice-skating parties, which had become seasonal events since the Central Park ponds were opened in the 1860's. These parties were popular not only as family outings, but also because they afforded young men and women an opportunity for courting—under the watchful eyes of parents. As one publication of the day pointed out, "the privilege a gentleman enjoys of imparting instruction in the art to his fair companion is to enjoy a combination of duty and pleasure not often within reach, and no relation is more calculated to produce tender attachments than that of pupil and tutor under such circumstances."

Decorating the home at Christmas time was a custom that went back to the days of ancient Rome, but it was raised to a new art in the late 1800's. In the weeks before Christmas, houses were festooned with bright, seasonal greenery, flowers, and decorations. One of the most favored flowers was the poinsettia, originally imported from Mexico, whose brilliant, red, leafy bracts represent the flaming star of Bethlehem.

By 1876, the centerpiece of any proper Christmas was a large, ornamented, evergreen tree set up inside the home. The Christmas tree was originally a German tradition. After England's Queen Victoria and her

Christmas shopping at a toy store on Broadway and Canal streets in New York City in 1865.

New Yorkers enjoy a winter day in an 1860's Currier and Ives lithograph, Central Park in Winter.

German husband, Prince Albert, set up a tree in Windsor Castle in 1841, the custom spread rapidly.

Decorating the tree and filling its boughs with presents was a very serious business, as one contemporary account of a New York doctor and his family shows: "Marian drew long strings of bright red holly berries threaded like beads upon fine cord, and festooned them in graceful garlands from the boughs which the Doctor had arranged with tiny candles. Long pieces of fine wire were passed through the candles at the bottom. These were clasped over the stem of each branch and twisted underneath, taking care to have a clear space above each wick so nothing might catch fire.

Strings of bright berries, small bouquets of paper flowers, strings of beads, tiny flags of gay ribbons, stars and shields of bright paper, lace bags filled with colored candies, knots of bright ribbons, all homemade, made a brilliant show. At last the more important presents were brought down from an upper room. Dolls for each of the little girls were seated on the boughs. A large cart for Eddie, with two horses prancing before it, drove gaily among the top branches. Beneath the branches Marian placed a set of wooden animals for Eddie, while from the topmost branch was suspended a gilded cage, ready for the canary bird purchased for the pet-loving Lizzie."

Christmas Eve was probably the busiest night of the year in most American homes. There was the last-minute wrapping of packages to be done and rushing a belated Christmas card across town to that old friend who had somehow been forgotten until his card arrived late in the afternoon. Many of the house decorations, too, waited until the 11th hour because there was an old belief that some Christmas greenery would bring misfortune to the family if brought into the house before Christmas Eve.

The night before Christmas was also a time for strolling bands, carolers, and handbell ringers who would come by to serenade each home with a rendition of such carols as "O Come, All Ye Faithful" or "It Came Upon a Midnight Clear." Each group would be invited inside for a glass of punch and perhaps given a few coins.

In a great many homes, it became a Christmas Eve tradition to gather the family together for a reading of the Charles Dickens classic story, *A Christmas Carol*. No writer ever loved Christmas more than Dickens,

A mother and her children admire their decorated Christmas tree in a wood engraving by John Whetten Ehninger (1827-1889).

and his tale of the redemption of Ebenezer Scrooge was felt to be a perfect reflection of the spirit of Christmas.

At long last, the young children were sent to bed after hanging their stockings for Santa Claus to fill later that night. Like the Christmas celebration itself, Santa Claus had not always been popular in all parts of America. Many concerned clergymen preached against Santa Claus from their pulpits because they feared that the emergence of such a folk culture would draw people's attention away from their celebration of the miracle of Christ's birth. But the idea of a jolly gift-giver from the North Pole proved to be too popular to be stamped out.

Christmas Day got started early as the children went through their stocking presents and eventually made such a din that the parents had to get up and go downstairs to open the presents under the tree. After breakfast, there might be a mid-morning church service, and then the family would walk back home for Christmas dinner.

There was an old English say-

An 1864 painting, Christmas-Time, The Blodgett Family, *by Eastman Johnson*

ing—the "the Devil himself dare not appear during Christmas for fear of being baked in a pie"—that could easily be applied to the United States in the 1800's. A typical Christmas dinner included a roast turkey with cranberry sauce, a boiled ham, goose pie, coleslaw, squash, beets, lemon custard, and a cranberry pie. In more elegant homes, dinner might include turtle soup, oyster pie, and a flaming plum pudding. The plum pudding would come last, its eerie blue flames casting strange shadows throughout the room. The pudding was dotted inside with small, silver coins that could be kept by whoever bit into one.

While the adults were still talking at the dinner table over nuts and candies, the children might steal away to another room to get ready to put on their own Christmas play for the family and guests. Once they were in costume and their props were in place, the rest of the household would be signaled to come to the parlor where they would watch the children offer a dramatic reading of "Twas the Night Before Christmas" complete with the sound of offstage sleigh bells and reindeer hooves.

After the play, the parlor would ring with the sounds of children's games as the whole family joined in "Blind Man's Bluff" and "Hunt-the-Slipper." Later that night there would be

An ardent gentleman tests the charm of mistletoe in an 1870's engraving.

one more Christmas cake—this one coated with marzipan and sugar. Finally, as it grew dark outside, the candles would be lit on the tree, and the family would gather around a piano to sing Christmas carols.

When we think about a traditional, "old-fashioned" American Christmas, this is the kind most turn to. And rightly so, for early Americans knew how to keep Christmas, and they established a holiday tradition that is as fresh today as it was more than a century ago. ❊

Season's Greetings

By the late 1870's, the sending of Christmas cards, which is now so much a part of the holiday tradition, was just gaining popularity. The first known Christmas card was designed in London, England, in 1843, by the illustrator John Callcott Horsley for a businessman named Sir Henry Cole.

It resembled a postcard and included space to write the names of the sender and the recipient. The card's design showed a happy family enjoying a Christmas celebration. Below the drawing, an inscription read, "Merry Christmas and a Happy New Year to You." Cole sold about 1,000 copies of the card. Since that time, the sending of greeting cards on special occasions has become an important social custom.

Although the first Christmas card designed and sent in the United States was likely produced as early as the 1850's, it was Louis Prang who popularized Christmas cards as we have come to know them. Prang, who came to the United States in 1850 from Breslau, Germany, is considered "the father of the American Christmas card." A superb craftsman, he developed a prosperous lithography business in Boston, and in 1875 he

A period Christmas tree decorates an interior at Maymont House (opposite), *a museum in Richmond, Virginia.*

began manufacturing the first Christmas cards in the United States. His early cards, delicately crafted, are masterpieces of lithography and were prized as works of art. Many other printers and publishers followed Prang's example, and Christmas cards began to gain in popularity in the United States. Although a few famous artists produced Christmas cards, more often anonymous or unknown artists designed them. Often, the cards' text quoted passages from the Bible, Shakespeare, or other famous literary works. Writers also wrote their own Christmas greetings for the cards.

Soon, American Christmas cards were available in a variety of designs, shapes, and styles. The cards became more ornate and were sometimes decorated with embossment, lace, or satin. Also popular were cards cut into three-dimensional shapes. Designs on the cards ranged from images of flowers, children, and pets, to religious symbols, such as angels, to illustrations of Santa Claus.

With improvements in mail service and printing, the sending and receiving of Christmas greeting cards became a more common part of the holiday tradition by the early 1900's—one that continues today. 🐚

Christmas cards, first introduced in England in the 1840's, quickly became as much a part of the season as Santa Claus and last-minute shopping.

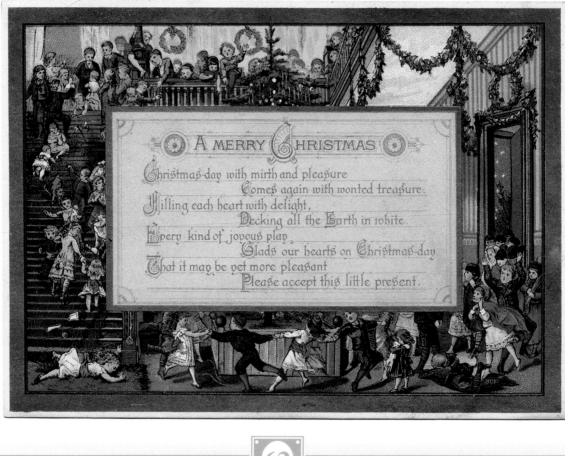

A MERRY CHRISTMAS

Christmas-day with mirth and pleasure
    Comes again with wonted treasure.
Filling each heart with delight,
    Decking all the Earth in white.
Every kind of joyous play
    Glads our hearts on Christmas-day.
That it may be yet more pleasant
    Please accept this little present.

A Collection of Historic Holiday Cards

A Happy Christmas to You!

A MERRY CHRISTMAS

YE CAROL.

A Merry CHRISTMAS AND A Happy New Year!

WISHING YOU A MERRY CHRISTMAS!

"Hang sorrow! Care will kill a cat,
And therefore let's be merry!"

The Season's Greetings

M. Humphrey

A Christmas Sampler

The Christmas holiday season in early America was both a time for relaxation and a period of furious activity. America was primarily a rural, agricultural nation in the 1700's and 1800's, and there were few people who could afford to take a summer vacation. Summer was the time for growing food and undertaking the construction projects that were so essential to the survival of a young nation. By the time winter set in, the crops had been harvested and the storing of provisions accomplished. Instead of settling down for a long winter's rest, many Americans found themselves caught up in the bustle of Christmas preparations. There were hunts to organize, parties to give, houses to decorate, and, of course, holiday dinners to prepare.

In the pages that follow, you will find several Yuletide decoration projects adapted for use today from the techniques of those early days. Some traditional colonial holiday recipes, brought up to date, are included as well. To add to your enjoyment of keeping a traditional Christmas, you will also find a selection of Christmas carols that Americans composed.

Harper's Weekly, *a leading publication of the 1800's, offered their readers this Christmas drawing in 1866.*

Pomander balls and sachets

These old-fashioned creations make delightful Christmas tree ornaments that are thoughtful presents as well. Once they have been used to decorate the tree or the table, they may be hung in your closet or placed in a bureau drawer. The scent of a pomander ball can last for years.

Sachets

A sachet is any small bag containing scented herbs or perfumed powders. You can experiment with these combinations as much as you like. This fragrant wood sachet is typical. Take ½ pound of sandalwood powder and ½ teaspoon of cedarwood oil and mix them together in a jar. Seal the jar tightly and let the mixture stand for a week. Make sachet bags by folding 4 by 8-inch pieces of cloth in half and sewing up each side as far as 1 inch from the top of the bag, about ½ inch in from the sides. Turn the sacks inside out. Any material may be used, but it should be woven tightly enough to hold the mixture. Fill the bags, gather the unsewn ends, and tie them tightly with ribbon.

Pomander balls

A thin-skinned orange is the usual start of a pomander ball, but almost any fruit can be used. A lemon makes a very attractive tree ornament.

Take an orange and stud it over its entire surface with whole cloves. You might need a skewer or heavy needle to make holes to get the cloves into the orange without breaking them. For decoration, the cloves can be loosely spaced, but the pomander ball will work better as a closet hanging if the surface is entirely covered with cloves. Once the fruit is studded, put it in a bowl containing a mixture of cinnamon, allspice, and orrisroot. Leave the fruit in the bowl for at least five days, and roll it around in the mixture twice a day.

When the fruit has dried out, put it in a piece of netting and tie it with a bow of velvet or satin ribbon.

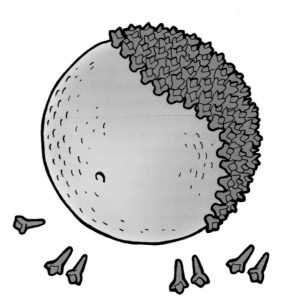

Patchwork project

It was an old colonial tradition to use bits of material from the family sewing box to create something new. Here are two projects that are simple to make and will provide bright Christmas time decorations for around the house.

Quilted Christmas stocking

Take any two pieces of brightly colored material and cut out a pair of identically sized stocking shapes. Place the stocking shapes on top of one another. Stitch around the sides of the stockings, but leave the top open. Turn the sewn stocking inside out. Stuff the stocking with Dacron fiberfill, cotton, or other loose cloth, cut to the shape of your stocking. Sew the top together by hand. With a darning needle, pull yarn through, making a square pattern, and knot tightly on each side of the stocking. Once you have made the basic stocking shape, you can decorate it with bells, tassels, decals, or anything you like. Remember though, this stocking is for decoration only. You will not get any presents in it.

Flying angel

Copy the patterns for the angel onto a large piece of paper with a 4-inch grid, and then cut them out. Pin the head, the halo, the wings, and the legs to a white material, and pin the arms and the body to a pink material. Cut the material around the patterns, allowing an extra ½ inch for seams. You will need two each of the material halo, head, feet, and arms. If you are going to put a dress on the angel, do so now. Then sew the angel's body and wings together. Cut a single piece of white material, identical in size and shape to the sewn body and wings, and sew the two pieces together, leaving openings for the arms and feet. Add stuffing. Next, partially sew the two sets of halos, heads, feet, and arms together, leaving a large enough opening to stuff. Draw the face on one of the white circles for the head. Stuff, sew, and attach all remaining pieces to the body and wings. Add a head of curls using yarn and a darning needle if you wish.

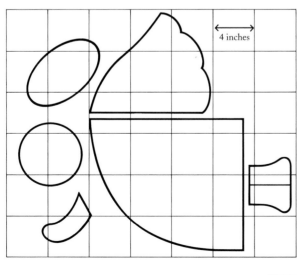

4 inches

Corn husk dolls

The early settlers in the American Colonies found that the corn stalk not only provided them with a new food but was also a resource for children who had to create their own toys. Making a corn husk doll is not as difficult as it may look. Essentially, it is just a simple cross decorated into the shape of a doll. Once you learn the basic form, you can shape these dolls into any position you like. They may be used on the tree as ornaments or given as presents.

To make a corn husk doll, you will need about 8 corn husks, 3 feet of florist's wire, an ounce of glycerin, and one soft rubber or Styrofoam ball about ³/₄-inch in diameter.

Spread the glycerin on the corn husks. Soak the corn husks in hot water for about 15 minutes until they are flexible.

To make the arms, cut off a 3-inch length of wire and cut one of the husks into a 1 by 4-inch rectangle. Lay the wire lengthwise in the middle of the husk and roll it up as tightly as you can, tying both ends with florist's wire (Fig. 1).

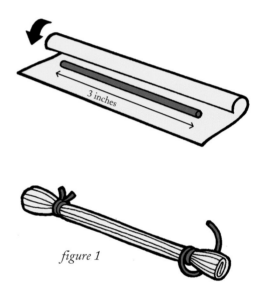

3 inches

figure 1

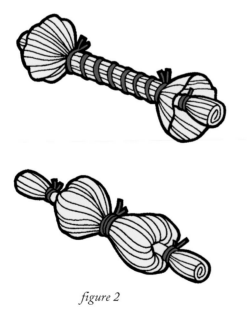

figure 2

Cut a second husk into the same size as the first, 1 by 4 inches. Make a 2-inch-long mark in the middle of a third husk. Wrap the third husk around the first one and wind securely with wire along the length of your mark. Now, take the ends of the second husk, fold them back to the middle, and secure them with wire (Fig. 2). Put aside.

To make the body, take a 4-inch piece of wire and stick it about halfway into the ball. This will form a base for the head. Attach the arms about an inch below the head and tie by wrapping wire around the neck and body several times. Make sure this basic form is secure and the rest will be easy.

Cut a 2 by 6-inch piece of husk and wire it around the head (Fig. 3). Bring the rest of the husk down and secure it to the wire about ½ inch below the arms. This makes the chest, which may be plumped out with cotton or any loose material. To make the shoulders, cut out two ½ by 4-inch pieces of husk and crisscross, wiring at the waist (Fig. 4).

figure 3   *figure 4*

To make the skirt, cut pieces of husks about 2 inches wide and at least 3 inches long. Wire them around the waist so that the husks reach above the doll's head (Fig. 5).

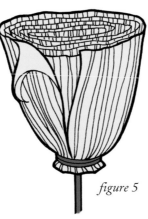

figure 5

You can bend the arms up so they are out of the way. Pull the layers of the skirt down one by one, smooth them, and trim them with scissors (Fig. 6).

Now the basic doll is complete. To finish the face, trim the husk around the head, and paint on the face. If you want to make a bonnet, attach a piece of husk to the head in any shape you like.

figure 6

Christmas Dinner

Christmas dinner in America has, since the earliest colonial days, reflected the native tastes and traditions of the country's forefathers and also included many of the unfamiliar foods early Americans found available in the New World.

For many years, the stern New Englanders kept Christmas in the simplest manner possible. In contrast, the Virginia cavaliers engaged in a week-long series of banquets and buffets. The plum puddings and mince pies of their English mother country were an important part of the ceremonies. One of the highlights of a Virginia Christmas was an invitation to Mount Vernon, where guests were treated to a sumptuous meal and several rounds of George Washington's incendiary eggnog.

In Baltimore, widely different ethnic backgrounds mingled during the colonial period, producing an Anglo-German tradition of serving a roast bird with sauerkraut. Early Dutch settlers in New York celebrated with masses of hearty food, especially on New Year's Day, when they held open house. Tables laden with baked hams, turkey, game birds, and lobster salad were set up, and doors were thrown open to any friend who wished to come in and toast the new year.

For a while, it was a common practice for New Yorkers to advertise in the local newspapers the times during which they would be receiving guests. They had to stop that, however, when startled hostesses found themselves entertaining total strangers who had read the papers and come by for a free meal.

In New Orleans, the Christmas season had a creole touch. The citizens of New Orleans, like the Dutch, saved their biggest celebrations for New Year's Day. A Louisiana New Year's dinner generally began with oysters and consommé, followed by fillet of sole stuffed with crab. Then the main course of roast turkey and yams, mashed potatoes, cauliflower, and salad was served, topped off with vanilla ice cream, flaming bananas, and that New Orleans specialty, *café brûlot*.

The New World provided an interesting collection of comestibles for the pioneers' Christmas table. Turkey and other native birds, and wild game—including squirrel, venison, buffalo, elk, antelope, prairie dog, and grizzly bear—often became a part of the newly come settlers' holiday fare. The Indians introduced cranberries and squash to them.

As the nation expanded westward, more combinations of the old and the new took root, eventually developing into unique regional holiday menus, all carrying on the American tradition of lavish Christmas hospitality.

The recipes in this section are all adapted from the traditional ones of the period and modernized for present-day cooking techniques.

George Washington's eggnog

This potent holiday drink was among the general's favorites. It is made in Virginia to this day, in exactly the same proportions. This recipe makes about three quarts.

1 pint brandy	4 ounces rum	1 quart milk
½ pint rye whiskey	12 eggs, separated	1 quart cream
4 ounces sherry	¾ cup sugar	

Combine liquors. Beat egg yolks in a large bowl until thick, then beat in sugar. Gradually add liquor, then milk and cream while continuing to beat. Beat egg whites to stiff, not dry, peaks; fold into liquid mixture. Cover and refrigerate for at least 5 days before serving.

Sorrel soup

Anyone fortunate enough to dine with Thomas Jefferson at Monticello might start with this simple but delicious cream soup. It can be served hot or ice cold. This recipe makes 4 to 6 servings.

1 pound fresh sorrel leaves	2 egg yolks, beaten	3 cups chicken broth
¼ cup butter	1 cup light cream	Salt and pepper to taste
1 medium onion, chopped		

Wash sorrel leaves thoroughly and then dry. Chop the leaves finely. Heat butter in a skillet, add onion, and cook until soft. Stir in sorrel and cook over low heat until wilted, about 5 minutes. Blend egg yolks and cream. Heat broth to boiling in a large saucepan. Stir a small amount of hot broth into egg yolk-cream mixture, then stir that mixture into broth and heat thoroughly. Add sorrel mixture and salt and pepper to taste. Serve hot or refrigerate until icy cold, and then serve. For a smoother soup, blend in an electric blender.

Baked ham and maple syrup

This is a dish that would likely be served at one of the New Year's Day receptions in a prosperous Dutch home in New York. An old-fashioned method of preparing ham, it is extremely simple. This recipe is for a single slice of ham that serves four, but it can be expanded into a buffet dish that serves several times that many. Asparagus or broccoli was usually served with it.

1 ham slice (1 ½ inches thick)	2 tablespoons cider vinegar
cloves (optional)	¾ cup maple syrup
2 teaspoons dry mustard	

Slash the fatty edge of ham several times to keep it from curling during cooking. Stud ham with cloves, if desired; put into a baking pan. Blend mustard, vinegar, and maple syrup; pour over ham. Bake at 350 °F about 1 hour, basting occasionally. Remove from oven. Transfer ham to a warm platter. Set the baking pan over high heat; cook and stir to reduce liquid to a sauce consistency. Pour over ham. Serve any extra sauce separately.

Baked stuffed fillets with creole sauce

This exotic offering was a great holiday favorite of New Orleans magnificos. Creole cooking is a spicy heritage from the original French and Spanish settlers of Louisiana. This example is quite rich, so if you prefer a simpler dish, don't stuff the fillets. Cook them according to your favorite recipe and serve with the sauce.

1/4 cup butter
2 tablespoons finely chopped onion
2 tablespoons chopped celery
2 tablespoons chopped green pepper
2 tablespoons flour

1/2 cup milk or light cream
1/4 teaspoon salt
1/8 teaspoon pepper
1/8 teaspoon paprika
2 teaspoons Worcestershire sauce
2 drops Tabasco sauce
1 cup cooked crab meat

1 cup cooked coarsely chopped shrimp
1/2 teaspoon chopped parsley
6 flounder or sole fillets
melted butter
creole sauce

Heat butter in a saucepan. Add onion, celery, and green pepper. Cook until ingredients are soft but not browned. Stir in flour and then milk. Cook and stir until thickened. Remove from heat; stir in seasonings, crab meat, shrimp, and parsley. Mound some stuffing on each fillet, roll up, and secure with wooden picks. Put the fillet roll-ups, leaving space between, into a greased shallow baking dish. Brush fish with melted butter. Bake at 350 °F for 10 to 15 minutes. Pour creole sauce over top of fish. Continue baking for 25 minutes. Makes 6 servings.

Creole sauce

4 cups canned or peeled fresh tomatoes
1 teaspoon salt
1/2 teaspoon thyme

1 bay leaf, crumbled
black and red pepper to taste

1 large clove garlic, finely chopped
2 tablespoons butter
1 tablespoon flour

Combine tomatoes, seasonings, and 1 tablespoon butter in a saucepan. Bring to a boil and cook over medium heat until sauce is reduced by half, stirring occasionally. Melt the remaining 1 tablespoon butter in a small saucepan. Blend in flour and cook over low heat until lightly browned. Mix with sauce and cook for 5 minutes.

Candied cranberries

2 cups fresh cranberries
1 cup sugar

Wash cranberries and spread over bottom of a shallow baking dish. Sprinkle with sugar and cover tightly. Bake at 350 °F for 1 hour, stirring occasionally. Chill before serving as a meat accompaniment.

New Orleans sweet potato pie

A traditional Southern Christmas dish, sweet potato pie has been called "sweet potatoes for people who hate sweet potatoes." Although it looks like a dessert, it is served as a vegetable.

4 eggs	¼ teaspoon salt	1 teaspoon vanilla extract
1 ½ cups mashed cooked sweet potatoes	⅔ cup milk	½ cup finely chopped pecans
	⅓ cup orange juice	1 unbaked 9-inch pastry shell
⅓ cup sugar	1 tablespoon honey	whipped cream topping

Beat eggs until foamy. Mix in sweet potatoes, then sugar, salt, milk, orange juice, honey, vanilla extract, and pecans. Pour mixture into pastry shell. Bake at 450 °F for 10 to 15 minutes. Turn oven regulator to 350 °F, and continue baking for about 25 minutes. Set on rack to cool. Spread whipped cream over top.

Moravian Christmas cookies

These spicy molasses cookies were a familiar treat at Moravian Christmas "Love Feasts." When they were made at times other than Christmas, they were much larger and were called cakes. This recipe makes about ten dozen thin cookies.

¼ cup lard	1 teaspoon cloves
¼ cup butter	¾ teaspoon ginger
1 cup molasses	¾ teaspoon baking soda
½ cup firmly packed brown sugar	3 ½ cups flour
1 teaspoon cinnamon	

Melt lard and butter together. Set aside to cool. Mix molasses and brown sugar in a bowl. Add melted fat and mix well. Blend spices, baking soda, and 1 tablespoon flour; stir into molasses mixture. Add the remaining flour. Refrigerate dough at least 4 hours. Roll out dough very thin on a floured surface. Cut into shapes and lay on greased cooky sheets. Bake at 350 °F for 8 to 10 minutes.

Café brûlot

A dazzling New Orleans specialty, this after-dinner drink was once described as "the crowning of a great dinner."

3 cups strong coffee	4 sticks cinnamon, broken in small pieces
½ large orange	1 ½ cups brandy or cognac
10 cubes sugar	
10 whole cloves	

Prepare coffee in your favorite manner; keep hot. Turn the orange half inside out and place, flesh side up, in an earthenware bowl or chafing dish. Add sugar, cloves, and cinnamon. Pour brandy (warmed, if not using chafing dish) over the orange. Ignite the brandy, then add the hot coffee. Ladle the liquid over the orange. Serve at once in demitasse cups. This recipe will make 16 servings.

American Carols

Most popular Christmas carols, and the custom of caroling itself, came from England. But the oldest recorded instance of caroling in America was French-inspired. In 1645, Father Barthélémy Vimont, S.J., reported that the Huron Indians at Mackinac (now Mackinaw, Michigan) met to "sing hymns in honor of the new-born Child." Another missionary of that time, Jean de Brébeuf, S.J., composed the first American carol, "Jesus is Born." It was written in the Huron language to the tune of an old French folk song.

America's best-known Christmas songs in English, however, have a much more recent origin. Edmund H. Sears, a Unitarian minister of Weston, Massachusetts, wrote the verse for "It Came Upon the Midnight Clear" in 1849, and Boston musician Richard S. Willis composed the rousing music the following year. In 1857, John Henry Hopkins, Jr., an Episcopalian minister, created both the words and the music for his classic carol "We Three Kings Of Orient Are."

In 1863, the famed poet Henry Wadsworth Longfellow watched with horror as the Civil War grew, taking the lives of thousands of young men on both sides. His own son had been seriously wounded fighting for the Union. Longfellow's poem, "I Heard the Bells on Christmas Day," was a plea for a speedy end to the bloody conflict. John Baptiste Calkin set it to music in 1872.

And in 1868, Phillips Brooks, later Episcopal Bishop of Massachusetts, wrote a poem for his Sunday School class inspired by a memory of a pilgrimage he had made to the Holy Land three years earlier. Lewis Redner set the poem to music, and it quickly became one of America's favorite Christmas songs…"O Little Town of Bethlehem."

American folk music has made its own unique contribution to the roster of home-grown carols. An odd offering from the Kentucky mountains claims, "Christ was born in Bethlehem, and Mary was his niece." And one of the loveliest of American Christmas hymns, "Rise Up, Shepherd, and Follow," originated with black slaves.

America's joyful Christmas sounds also draw heavily on the heritage of the many immigrants—the Irish, the Germans, the Italians, the Poles, and others who brought their favorites with them across the sea.

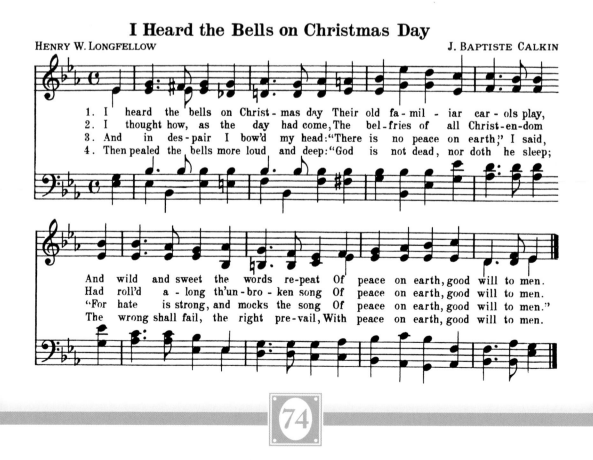

I Heard the Bells on Christmas Day

HENRY W. LONGFELLOW

J. BAPTISTE CALKIN

1. I heard the bells on Christ-mas day Their old fa-mil-iar car-ols play,
2. I thought how, as the day had come, The bel-fries of all Christ-en-dom
3. And in des-pair I bow'd my head:"There is no peace on earth," I said,
4. Then pealed the bells more loud and deep:"God is not dead, nor doth he sleep;

And wild and sweet the words re-peat Of peace on earth, good will to men.
Had roll'd a-long th'un-bro-ken song Of peace on earth, good will to men.
"For hate is strong, and mocks the song Of peace on earth, good will to men."
The wrong shall fail, the right pre-vail, With peace on earth, good will to men.

It Came upon the Midnight Clear

EDMUND H. SEARS

RICHARD S. WILLIS

1. It came up-on the mid-night clear, That glo-rious song of old, __
2. Still thro' the clo-ven skies they come, With peace-ful wings un-furled;
3. O ye be-neath life's crush-ing load, Whose forms are bend-ing low, __
4. For lo! the days are has-t'ning on, By proph-ets seen of old, __

From an-gels bend-ing near the earth, To touch their harps of gold: __
And still their heav'n-ly mu-sic floats O'er all the wea-ry world:
Who toil a-long the climb-ing way With pain-ful steps and slow; __
When with the ev-er-cir-cling years Shall come the time fore-told, __

"Peace on the earth, good will to men From heav'n's all gra-cious King," __
A-bove its sad and low-ly plains They bend on hov-'ring wing, __
Look now, for glad and gold-en hours Come swift-ly on the wing; __
When the new heav'n and earth shall own The Prince of Peace their King, __

The world in sol-emn still-ness lay To hear the an-gels sing. __
And ev-er o'er its Ba-bel sounds The bless-ed an-gels sing. __
Oh rest be-side the wea-ry road And hear the an-gels sing. __
And the whole world send back the song Which now the an-gels sing. __

We Three Kings Of Orient Are

J. H. H. Jr.

JOHN H. HOPKINS JR.

Kings. 1. We three kings of O - ri - ent are, Bear - ing gifts we trav - erse far
Melchior. 2. Born a babe on Beth-le-hem's plain, Gold we bring to crown Him a - gain;
Casper. 3. Frank-in-cense to of - fer have I; In - cense owns a De - i - ty nigh,
Balthazar. 4. Myrrh is mine; its bit - ter per - fume Breathes a life of gath - 'ring gloom;
All. 5. Glo-rious now be - hold Him rise, King and God and Sac - ri - fice;

far Field and foun - tain, moor and moun - tain, Fol - low-ing yon - der Star.
gain; King for - ev - er, ceas-ing nev - er, O - ver us all to reign.
nigh, Pray'r and prais-ing all men rais - ing, Wor - ship God on high.
gloom; Sorrow-ing, sigh - ing, bleed-ing, dy - ing, Sealed in the stone - cold tomb.
fice; Heav'n sings "Hal - le - lu - jah!" "Hal - le - lu - jah!" earth re - plies.

CHORUS

Oh, star of won - der, star of might, Star with roy - al beau - ty bright,

West-ward lead - ing, still pro - ceed - ing, Guide us to the per - fect light.

O Little Town of Bethlehem

PHILLIPS BROOKS

LEWIS H. REDNER

1. O lit - tle town of Beth - le - hem, How still we see thee lie;
2. For Christ is born of Ma - ry; And gath - ered all a - bove,
3. How si - lent - ly, how si - lent - ly, The won - drous gift is giv'n!
4. O ho - ly Child of Beth - le - hem, De - scend to us, we pray;

A - bove thy deep and dream - less sleep The si - lent stars go by:
While mor - tals sleep, the an - gels keep Their watch of won - d'ring love.
So God im - parts to hu - man hearts The bless - ings of His heav'n.
Cast out our sin, and en - ter in, Be born in us to - day.

Yet in thy dark streets shin - eth The ev - er - last - ing Light;
O morn - ing stars, to - geth - er Pro - claim the ho - ly birth;
No ear may hear His com - ing, But in this world of sin,
We hear the Christ - mas an - gels The great glad tid - ings tell;

The hopes and fears of all the years Are met in thee to - night.
And prais - es sing to God, the King, And peace to men on earth.
Where meek souls will re - ceive Him, still The dear Christ en - ters in.
O come to us, a - bide with us, Our Lord Em - man - u - el.

Index

Acknowledgements

Cover WORLD BOOK photo by Dale Debolt
(© Brunschwig & Fils); © The Stock Solution

2 Library of Congress

6 © Ellen K. Rudolph

8 © Corbis/Bettmann

9-10 Colonial Williamsburg Foundation

11 © Kelly-Mooney, Corbis

12 Smithsonian Institution

13 Mary Evans Picture Library/Alamy Images

14 Granger Collection

15 New York Public Library Picture Collection

16 Old Salem Museum, Winston-Salem, NC;

18 Metropolitan Museum of Art, New York City, Gift
of John Stewart Kennedy, 1897

20 Abby Aldrich Rockefeller Folk Art Museum,
Colonial Williamsburg Foundation

21 Shelburne Museum;
Colonial Williamsburg Foundation

22 Abby Aldrich Rockefeller Folk Art Museum,
Colonial Williamsburg Foundation

23 Colonial Williamsburg Foundation;
Shelburne Museum

24 Northwind Picture Archives

26 The Clymer Family and the Clymer Museum of Art

27 Culver Pictures

28 Edward W. & Bernice Chrysler Garbisch Collection

29 WORLD BOOK map

30 Museum of the City of New York,
The Harry T. Peters Collection

31 Museum of Fine Arts, Boston, Gift of
Martha C. Karolik for the M & M Karolik Collection
of American Painting

32 New York Public Library Picture Collection

35 Library of Congress

36 Colonial Williamsburg Foundation

37 © Kelly-Mooney, Corbis; Greenfield Village &
Henry Ford Museum, Dearborn, MI;
Colonial Williamsburg Foundation

38 Colonial Williamsburg Foundation

39 Colonial Williamsburg Foundation;
© Ellen K. Rudolph

40 American Greetings from Antique & Collectible News

42 Smithsonian Institution

44 *Harper's Weekly*

46 Smithsonian Institution

47-49 *A Visit from St. Nicholas* by Clement C. Moore, with
original woodcuts by Boyd, 1848

51 *Harper's Weekly;* Library of Congress

52 Maymont House Museum
(photo by Dennis McWaters)

54 New York Public Library Picture Collection

55 Historical Pictures Service

56 © Superstock

57 *The Christmas Tree*, Museum of Fine Arts,
Boston, Gift of W. G. Russell Allen

58 Metropolitan Museum of Art, Gift of
Mr. & Mrs. Stephen Whitney Blodgett

59 *Under the Mistletoe* from an engraving, 1869,
Dover Publications

60 © Jeff Greenberg, Alamy Images

62 Livaudais Collection

63-64 Hallmark Cards, Inc.; Livaudais Collection

65 New York Public Library Prints Division

70 Colonial Williamsburg Foundation

Craft Illustrations: Product Illustration Inc.*

Recipe Cards: Eileen Mueller Neill*

Advent Calendar: © The Stock Solution

Advent Calendar Illustrations: Laura D'Argo*

All entries marked with an asterisk (*)
denote illustrations created exclusively for
World Book, Inc.

*The printed textile used on the cover of this book
and throughout its pages is from an English toile
produced by Bromley Hall Printworks between
1765 and 1795.*